HOW TO FIX THE REALITY
WE CREATED

BRANDON OLSEN

Table of Contents

Introduction

In this book, we will go over how we create reality at an individual level, how we create at a collective level, how we co-create reality, and how to fix the collective reality. This information came to me as I was prompted to write this book. After receiving this information, I spent roughly one year refining it. Refining the information was necessary because every person has an ego. When someone channels information from the other side, it is filtered through their ego. Ego in this case is my perspective. I ensured every part of the book resonates truth with me.

This book intends to provide a foundational level understanding of reality creation. I am not saying this is how reality works for everyone, as we all create reality differently. However, there are many commonalities and universal laws that many of us agree upon. Everything in this book should be taken as a suggestion to help you become a better person. I am doing my part to bring more love into the world, and I am sure many of you are doing the same. Thank you for reading my book and thank you for being a good person.

The perspective I choose to have in this experience involves a higher power. A source of creation. My preferred term for the source of creation is God. I also use the term God for all that is. There are many terms for the Divine Source; some of which I will use throughout the text. You know the term you like to use. I believe we are all talking about the same thing in different ways. We all have our own perspectives and the perspectives in this book should open you up to going within to see what resonates with you.

Chapter 1
How We Create Reality

"All that we are arises from our thoughts," a famous translation of the words spoken by Gautama Buddha. I interpret this translation to mean we create our reality based on what we choose to think about. Our thoughts become our words, and our words in turn become our actions. The thoughts we choose to think about are the ones we end up allowing to come to fruition. These are the thoughts we select and put our attention on. Think of the human body as a computer. Our eyes see the screen. Everything else comes from within. We choose what we see. If we decide to switch to another webpage, we click another webpage. If we decide to see something else, we turn our head to see something else. We are now viewing a different page. We are now viewing a different area. When you click on a webpage you put your attention there. Google will place ads with similar information for you to see. As you focus your attention on certain aspects of life, similar events and circumstances will arise. Think about where you are sitting as you are reading this book. Stop for a second and look around. This is the setting you have chosen to be in as you read this. You could have chosen to sit in any room of your house, any building in your town, anywhere outside, any part of the state or country you live in, but you have chosen to be wherever you are. Every choice you made in life manifested events and circumstances that led you here. Where you are now is the foundation of the reality you are creating. The past lives only in your mind, as well as the future. Where you focus your attention will direct your life.

Now that we are aware of the physical foundation of the reality we reside in, we can ponder on our thoughts. Where do they come from? What is their purpose? Why do we have them? Where these thoughts come from is from wherever you believe they come from, as none of us know exactly where the thoughts arise from. I believe that thoughts come to me from God and the other beings that God has created. We will shed more light on this subject in the next chapter.

Our thoughts give us prompts on what to do. We think about certain things, talk about certain things, and eventually, do certain things. Ultimately, what we do comes from thought. There is also the question of who came up with those thoughts. Was it you? Was it someone who talked to you about the topic? Did they place thoughts in your mind? This coincides with co-creation. I will dive deeper into co-creation in the next chapter. Wherever your thoughts come from, or whatever reason you have the thought, it is there. Why do you have thoughts in your head? Well, I believe we have them because we are meant to act on them. Of course, we have a choice on whether we want to act on our thoughts, as there are many different ones in our heads. Perhaps it is the most recurring thoughts that are meant to be acted upon, or perhaps those epiphany thoughts we should act upon. The thoughts given the most attention are the ones we manifest through our decision to act on them.

The goal for those of us reading this book is to help ourselves and others in the course of our spiritual journey by becoming more aware of the decisions we choose to make. This book provides perspectives that activate a better way of living. Take what resonates with you and show others a better way of living. Show them how to heal so that they can work on the foundation in which they manifest from. When we generate more positive thoughts for ourselves, we help others generate more positive thoughts by being near them. Continue to lead by example and find ways to show or tell others that they can choose where to place their focus. They will wake up when the time is right. They will begin to consciously choose their thoughts, words, and actions.

Once we have decided the thoughts to pursue, our bodies begin working to bring the thoughts to life. For those of us who meditate, we ponder on our thoughts before deciding on which to pursue. Others stay in a continual state of motion, always thinking about what to do next before completing the task at hand. Many of us do both. Some of us meditate without the awareness that we are meditating — I'm talking about the daydreamers out there. You do not have to sit or lay in any specific way to meditate; although, I do believe that certain positions allow for better flow during meditation.

When it comes to creating reality, the thoughts we have become our words, and our words in turn become our actions. Our thoughts are exclusive to us until we share them or decide not to act on them. Some thoughts fizzle away if not acted upon. Others, however, such as divine ideas will be sent to another. When we have a divine idea, we have a choice to create or dismiss them. If we do not act upon the divine idea we are given, God will place the idea in another expression of Himself. Have you ever had a moment where you thought of some brilliant idea but never acted upon it? Then, a year later, you see someone making millions of dollars from that same idea you had. I would consider these thoughts to be divine ideas for us to pursue. These divine ideas could also be called God's desires; ideas that God will manifest into our lives if we choose to manifest them. Many of these ideas reoccur in our minds until we decide to take the step to bring them to life. When we decide to manifest the idea, it is as if we open a door to infinite possibilities.

Now we have our foundation and a thought process about where our thoughts come from. Let's dive into preexisting beliefs. When we were children, our parents taught us how life works; meanwhile, it is possible that they were ignorant as to how life truly works. They were told how life works by their parents and the people in charge of the world. The belief of how the world works is created by everyone in the world. But then again, not all of us believe in the same thing. Many of us believe in specific things — Christians, Buddhists, Hindus, and so on and so forth. We even have scientists who are trying to find a way to explain how the world works. Some believe we go to heaven; some believe we are reincarnated, and there are others who believe something else. We all believe in something. For me, I believe we live in heaven. Heaven is what we make it. Heaven is a word I like to use for the simulation many of us believe to be living in. The term "heaven" creates a positive feeling associated with simulation. We can create whatever it is that we would like in heaven. We will always be in heaven. We go through many lives in many ways so that we have something to do throughout our eternal existence.

So, why are we here? I have come to four purposes for our existence so far: expansion, experience, growth, and perspective. God could not see Himself from another perspective until He created us. The big bang perspective provides insight into the release of energy that was God creating many different expressions of Himself. We are all divine expressions of God, and we will continue to experience all that God knows for our soul growth, and in order to have something to do. As our souls grow, Spirit expands. We will make a difference between "soul" and "Spirit" for better understanding. Spirit is all of everything — God, as I like to call Him. For now, let's view Spirit as an ocean. The soul is an individual expression of Spirit. We could call a soul a drop in the ocean. The ocean is water, and the drop is water. The soul is created in the likeness of Spirit, and we are created in the likeness of God, therefore, we are God. Each of us is a perspective of experience. God is formless, aside from His creations and their creations. He has given us a form. God is always expanding with our growth and His new creations. Each creation has its own perspective of life. Each drop of water sees a different perspective of the ocean; perspectives that would not be seen if the ocean was not created. Thanks to God, we get to experience life.

Why did God give us the gift to experience life? In the last paragraph, I explained expansion and growth. Let's dive deeper into experience and perspective. We will get on to my reasoning behind believing we are in heaven in the next passage. In the beginning, God was all there was. This time let's equate God to the knowingness of all that could ever be, knowingness for short. The knowingness longed to experience what it knew. However, this knowingness had no way to experience what it knew. So, the knowingness divided itself up into all of us. Each of us is a piece of knowingness. All of us get to experience what the knowingness already knows. We came up with names for this knowingness. My favorite is "God." God has always been here. What is "here"? "Here" is relative to each expression of God. An expression of God includes me, you, the tree, the flower, the table, and everything around us. Each with their own definition of "here". So, what is "here"? If we each have a different perspective, what is "here"? This is something only God has an exact understanding of, for God sees everything from each experience. Being able to see everything, He has every perspective of "here." With every perspective, He can see the whole picture. I see a small portion of the picture, you see a different small portion of the picture, the tree sees a different small portion, and so on and so forth. With this, we can explain who created "here" as a being who lives through all of us; that we are all one being living life from many perspectives all for the sake of experience. Through us, He gets to experience what He knows. We decide the aspects of knowingness that get experienced. We always create "here" with our thoughts. Each perspective of "here" also has a perspective of God. This allows God to see Himself through our eyes. To answer the question of what is "here"? "Here" is God. God is everything. The kingdom of heaven is "here." The kingdom of heaven is God.

To further elaborate on why I believe we live in heaven, we will talk about some quotes from the Holy Bible; quotes from Jesus himself. In John 3:3, Jesus states, "I say unto thee, except a man be born again, he cannot see the kingdom of God." In John 3:5-6, Jesus says "Very truly I tell you, no one can enter the kingdom of God unless they are born of water and the Spirit. Flesh gives birth to flesh, but the Spirit gives birth to spirit." My interpretation of this is that being born from a womb equates to being born of water. Going through a spiritual awakening equates to being born of Spirit. Spiritual awakening can also be called enlightenment. It is not a secular event, but a process. Yes, there is a singular event where one is born again. However, this begins the process where one can see their ego, id, and superego. The removal of the ego and id is impossible. Looking at other terms of the three components of our being, we find body, mind, and soul, with ego being body, id being mind, and superego being soul. When one fully reaches enlightenment, one learns how to vibrate in harmony with their ego and id. Vibrating in harmony with the ego and id means they are still a part of us, though we are the super ego, or the soul, if you prefer to view things in the body, mind, and soul terms. These are things we will always have in a body. We can choose which processes to align with. In choosing to align with our souls, we perceive our world from a state of divinity, thus allowing us to see the kingdom of heaven and helping us realize that we are one with everything seen and unseen. We are here to help each other learn and grow spiritually. We each have something that we will do, so, we should not compare ourselves to others. We should express our divinity within and show the world who we are. We should also tell people what we think. Our thoughts and ideas matter, for no one can fully comprehend what is going on in the universe while residing in it. We are meant to live and experience life. We are here to create. We can create anything. I mean, look at Elon Musk who is launching rockets into space and landing them back on Earth. 100 years ago, no one would have believed it would be possible to travel into outer space, let alone land back on Earth. Yet, Elon had the thought and brought it into reality. I am not saying that Elon Musk is enlightened; what I am saying is he has found his passion and is living his truth. He stands strong in his thoughts and beliefs while also being open to new ideas. He understands that he has much he can teach, but he also understands that others can teach him. All of us are teachers. We each have something to contribute to society; something unique to us. We are also all students, meeting specific people along our paths who teach us what we need to know. This reality we are experiencing is what I believe to be heaven. Each of us gets to experience it how we decide to.

Now, we have the foundation, thoughts, and beliefs. We have something to talk about and agree upon with other sentient beings. Sentient means they have thoughts they can act upon. Whether or not these beliefs are true, we believe them to be. I mentioned ego earlier. Ego is an acronym for "edging God out."

Feeling separate from God when we are always one. I equate ego to the individual's perceived reality. Becoming enlightened, we remove the belief that reality works in the way we think it does. We realize that we know very little of how things work; we were limited to the ways others have told us as well as the way we think it does. Now, we are open to new possibilities, and see the world from new perspectives. Some perspectives you may agree with, others, you may not. Take what resonates with you and leave the rest.

Everyone has thoughts. These thoughts shape the reality we perceive. Let's think about different cultures. Beliefs vary from culture to culture. Individuals from different cultures live in different areas, they do not interact with one another. They experience a completely different reality. They speak a different language, have different customs, and live in a different environment. We may never have learned different ways of living if humans had not decided to explore the planet. There are many different religions out there. Once we remove dogma, my way is the only way, we begin to receive insight from the beliefs of others. At least allowing them to speak and hearing the wisdom they have to share. Then, you realize that there is much more going on than what is in your bubble. Your bubble is not a bubble; it is an intersection on an exceptionally large net. Each crossing point, or intersection, is an individual perception of reality. Each point is connected to another to create reality. This section of the net may look different than the section on the other half of the world. We can also talk about the belief that we have to pay taxes for the land we were born on. We could talk about the belief that you are prettier than her. There are so many different beliefs out there. All these beliefs help shape reality. The clothes we wear, the way we walk, the way we talk, and what we believe is appropriate and inappropriate, have all been decided upon by the sentient beings residing in a region.

With the understanding of how we choose what we do, how others have different realities, and how we all have different beliefs, we can now talk about how we create our reality. Back to what Buddha said, "All that we are arises from our thoughts." Everything we experience starts as a thought. If there was only one person on this planet, that person could create anything. If they believed they could do magic, then they could do magic. Yes, this is possible. Absolutely everything comes from belief. However, there is not only one person on Earth, and according to what we have been told, magic is not real. We have been given a pre-existing belief. We have also been told that psychics are nonsense, although more people are becoming aware of psychic abilities. Those of you reading this book are probably aware of psychic abilities. You may even have some of these abilities yourself. We are all psychic; it is just a matter of believing you are. However, being a psychic may not be your role in this life, just as being a carpenter may not be your role.

We are starting to understand many "truths" we have been told are not true. Now, we understand that we can change the reality we reside in, and how to create it.

Here is an example within the current belief of reality:

Timmy decides at a young age that he will be a doctor. All his life, he studies medicine. Of course, he goes through traditional school, learning basic education with other kids his age. Timmy's focus is on medicine. He thinks about medicine daily. He watches medical shows on TV, decides what college to go to, what classes to take, what medical school to go to, what internship, what residency, and what hospital to work at.

Every choice he made created the reality he experienced. Had he chosen not to go into healthcare, he would not have met his best friend, Trevor. If he decided to be a musician, he have made different friends. He also would not have gone to school for as long. He would have created a different reality to experience.

Now, we can go even deeper:

Timmy is in medical school. He has a decision to go out with friends or stay home and study. Timmy decides to go out. He meets the love of his life. Had he stayed home and studied, he may not have met her. He also decided how to approach her, what he said to her and where to look on her body.

He chose every aspect of what he experienced. He made every decision. He created the reality he is living in. Had he decided to be a musician, a different girl may have come along; or perhaps the same girl also decided to be a musician. She too created her reality. The point is, we decide every aspect of our lives. Now, the question is, where do the choices we decide upon come from? Where do we get the thought to say this? Why do we decide to do this? Why did I decide to write a book?

Chapter 2
How We Co-Create Reality

In the last chapter, we covered how we create reality at an individual level. We also asked the question of where our thoughts come from. Our thoughts could only be generated from two places. One is from external events that happen in our lives. External includes our thoughts, emotions, feelings, words spoken by ourselves and others, and anything we experience through our senses. There are many senses, only some of which are perceived. All of these are external experiences. An internal experience on the other hand, is solely observing all that is perceived through the individual expression that is me. However, this is not the second place in which we receive thoughts. Now that we have a difference between external and internal experience. What is the other way thoughts are generated?

The other source would be original. I believe our original thoughts come from our creator. We co-create reality with a higher being. This higher being is us, and we are it. We are all one, able to communicate with all parts of ourselves. Every person and being in this plane is creating the collective reality. There is also the perspective of all that is that created us. I am one drop in the ocean of all that is. This highest perspective is one drop of all that is — two very differently-sized drops of the same thing. To understand this, I will allude to "Conversations with God." God tells us in Neale Donald Walsch's book that there is no end to Him. God describes the use of a high-powered microscope to view a cell, and how we can continue to split the smallest particle of matter infinitely. There is no smallest particle in this sense. We can also do this the other way, infinitely, in the sense of God. We are one cell in the body of God. There is no highest level of perception. It is infinitely higher. I recommend reading "Conversations with God," if you would like to understand this more. My point in sharing this is to say that God is all. Every single perspective in the infinite number of perspectives is God. The word "God" in this case means everything; oneness of everything seen and unseen. The original source of our thoughts is God. We are God. All is God. These thoughts are the ones we call our intuition, listening to the Holy Spirit, divine insight, and so on and so forth. Whatever we call it, it comes from Source. In Christianity, there is an understanding of God's helpers; that they help us throughout our lives, and they speak to us all the time if we are open to hearing. Some of them are angels, some of them are the beings you have come to know. Ultimately, they are all expressions of God, and we are the ones who have given them names.

We can communicate with these beings through prayer and meditation. They can communicate with us whenever they need to. A conscious example of angelic help is hearing what to do. For example, you hear "go to the mall." You have a choice whether or not to listen. I had this happen to me on Black Friday. I decided to listen, and I headed to the mall. On the way there, I was given directions I would not normally go. Turn here, turn there, I listened and kept driving. I got to the mall with no intention of buying anything. I asked, "where do I go?" And I was instructed to "walk around." I walked around the crowded mall and was told to go into a store I would not normally go into. I decided not to listen and kept walking. I was then told, "turn around and go into the store." So, I turned around and walked into the store. I saw my first love working there. I figured I would be talking to her, but I was told to shop around. I found a shirt that read, "stop and smell the roses." The girl I was talking to at the time used that phrase and helped me to slow down and enjoy the present moment. I was told to buy the shirt. It was the last one, and it was her size. I did not end up talking to my first love. I walked out of the store and asked, "where do I go now?" I heard, "home," so, I began walking towards the exit.

As soon as I got outside, the girl I was talking to drove by with her windows down. We made eye contact as she was singing. She turned to park, and I walked out to her car. I told her about my experience and how every second counts in this reality; that we get to listen and go with the flow. Then, I hugged her, gave her the shirt, and she went to deliver food. She was door-dashing and had multiple orders. So, I went back to my car and headed home. An hour later, she sent a text, telling me about seeing her first love at the mall. I called her and we talked about the synchronicities in our experiences. Had I not listened to the internal prompt of "go to the mall," none of this would have happened. It was such a wonderful experience for us to have. An example of unconscious communication with higher beings would be when you accidentally turn at a stoplight when you were supposed to go straight. You turn around to get back on track and you see an accident occurred right where you would have been. These beings changed your thought processes so that you would turn, possibly saving your life. Another example would be losing your keys, only to find them in the first place you looked. The amount of time you spent looking around allowed you to run into your old friend at the gas station. Everything happens for a reason, and these helpers have a lot to do with what is going on here. All we have to do is listen to these higher thoughts and go with the flow, knowing and trusting that all is well, and everything is always in divine order.

There are many aspects of how we create our reality within these two sources — more than I will mention in this book. This book provides a foundational understanding. Let's dive into karma, dharma, and the law of attraction. These aspects are ever-present in everything we do. Because what I talk about in this book requires very little understanding of these topics to understand what I am saying, I will briefly touch on these topics.

I like to explain karma the way I did to my preschool students; it is simple, yet effectively gets the point across. I had a student who was fighting and being mean to other students. So, one day, I asked him to come to my desk. I told him I was going to show him how karma works. I had been telling many of my students about karma, so he was familiar with me saying, "karma will get you." I went on to give him a visual representation of how karma works. I grabbed two trays and some markers, and labeled one tray good karma, and the other tray, bad karma. Then, I said "Gavin, you have hit 10 kids today and said 5 mean things. I will put 15 markers into your bad karma pile. On the other hand, you have said 4 nice things to your friends today. I will put 4 markers in the good karma pile. Now, let's look at the other side of karma. You have 15 bad things that will happen to you in your life. You have 4 good things that will happen to you in your life. If I were to add yesterday's total, we will say is also 15 bad karma markers, then that puts you at 30 bad things that will happen in your life from these 2 days. 8 good things. Now, let's add up the whole week. One whole week with 15 bad markers a day makes 105 bad things that will happen in your life. 28 good things. Gavin, I know you may not understand everything I am saying, but you do understand that more bad than good is going to happen in your life. You can change this by being nice to people." I then proceeded to show him how to give compliments, as well as how to do nice things for his classmates. He was much nicer afterwards. What you put into your life is what you get out of it — this is how karma works.

Now, with an understanding of karma, we can talk about dharma. Dharma essentially means the code of your life's purpose. Your moral code you are meant to live by. You gain positive karma when you make positive choices that are in line with your moral code. If you stray away from your life's purpose by making negative choices, then you gain negative karma, all of which will be returned to you. I prefer to have good things come my way. So, I ensure every choice I make is in alignment with my morals. Some people may not always agree with your choices, and this brings me to the law of attraction.

You attract what you put into the world. It is similar to karma, meaning that you get what you put into the world. The difference between karma and the law of attraction is karma accounts for past actions creative power, while the law of attraction focuses on the present moment. Both deal with your thoughts, feelings, and beliefs. You will attract like-minded people, you will attract what you feel worthy of, and you will attract what you feel in general. If you feel like a millionaire, you will attract money. This is easier said than done. If you are persistent, consistent, and understand how to create reality, it can be done with ease. This goes for anything you feel you are. You will attract what you feel. However, you can live an incredibly positive karmic life and still have negative things happening to you. This can come from you not feeling worthy of positive things in your life. It could come from thoughts you had before certain events, that were worrisome. Perhaps you had some negative thoughts that created a negative event. All of our thoughts are creative. If there are negative thoughts in your head, you might manifest negative things in your life. On the other hand, some of us stay positive 99 percent of the time and still have negative things happen. Where do these come from? Well, there is an acronym for "fate" that I like — From All Thoughts Everywhere. I got the acronym from "Conversations with God." From All Thoughts Everywhere means that other sentient beings in your reality help to shape your reality. If your mother is a worrier, her worries may manifest in your life. If a classmate wishes you harm, their wishes may manifest. This is why it is best to surround yourself with loving people. It is also important to lead by example and bring understanding to those who are unaware. Another possibility of negative things is that we chose for them to happen before living this life. This means that while we were in a spiritual plane, we decided on some of the events that would happen in this experience of life, all for the purpose of experience. We will expound on the spiritual plane perspective in the next chapter.

Focusing on the individual expressions that we are, we have thoughts, feelings, emotions, and other external senses that create reality. Emotion is the way the body reacts to the image you see, or what happens to your body. Feelings are the consciousness of having emotions. I have a good feeling about this. Our feelings create reality, as well as our thoughts. When I feel as though a certain thing will happen, I create a belief that it will happen. The more thoughts surround this feeling, the more likely it is brought to existence. This does not mean every feeling will be brought into reality, as there are other sentient beings with thoughts and feelings residing in your space. If everyone feels the same way, that is what will be created. If the group of people all have different feelings, it is a "majority rules" affair as to what will be created. Let's say 4 out of 7 people believe this will happen, so that is what happens. However, this may not always be the case. We have more than 7 people on Earth. Perhaps more people that are not in the room believe differently, so, we have thoughts and feelings creating the reality we see. Each of us has our own reality, but collectively, we create the known reality. We also know there are patterns to how we create reality. Universal laws we have come to agree upon. Using these laws, we gain an understanding of how and what we are creating, as well as what our true desires are.

Going back to the example of having 7 people in a room, let's refer to this as a coven of witches. They gather together so that their collective thoughts become more easily manifested. When people of like minds come together, the area they reside in is more in alignment with their thoughts. If you live in the U.S. and you are on a spiritual path, you have most likely heard of a town called "Sedona" in Arizona. This town is full of psychic readers, crystal shops, energy healers, you name it. So many people in Sedona believe in something more than this physical reality. This area having so many people of like minds is a wonderful place to manifest. If you were to go to a city such as New York City, your manifestation may take longer to come to fruition. However, whoever you are, and wherever you are, you are right where you are meant to be at this moment in time, and you are creating reality at your pace. Through meditation, you will find what direction you would like to go, what you desire to manifest, and what truly makes you happy.

Now that we know our thoughts create reality, where do they come from? Do they magically pop into our heads? Do we create those too? They come from somewhere. I believe they come from God. Again, this is my preferred term for the supreme being who created us and is everything. I think the Divine Source gives us choices to pick from, and we are given free will. We decide the thought to act upon. Think of it like a multiple-choice test, except that this time, you have multiple actions to select for the body you reside in. You choose what the body says and does. Your thoughts would be the prompts you select from. What to feel is also a prompt you can select. Where do the prompts come from? To me, this means someone, or something is giving us choices to pick from. So, the answer to this question is the prompts come from Source. God created us, so, both ways, we derive thoughts would come from God. Saying that God gives us thoughts does not mean we only make good decisions; we have free will, and we are here to experience. There is no good or bad, there only is.

Now, we have a good understanding of how we create reality with our thoughts, feelings and emotions, and an idea of where they come from. Where do we go from here? We will talk about first principles to help us figure out where to go next. The way Aristotle defined first principles is "the first basis from which a thing is known." This is the way most scientists think. They do not assume anything. They ask, "what do we know to be true?" Then, they go from there. What they know to be true would be the first principle — where they start. For them, it could be the chemical composition of one or multiple materials they are using; it could just be the materials they are using for the experiment. They do not always go that deep. The reason I am talking about science and the first principle is to attribute the first principle to our thoughts. This is where we start a decision-making process. My question at the beginning of the chapter was, "where do our thoughts come from?" I am bringing the first principle into this to look at the facts. The facts are, we have thoughts, they come from somewhere, and we make decisions based on these thoughts. The rest is left to interpretation. There is no way to prove where the thoughts come from. We as humans will not be able to determine an exact science of how we co-create reality. However, we can look at events in our lives suggesting this. What events happen in our lives that suggest co-creation? The way I view life is somewhat planned by the Divine Source, like a movie script allowing the actors to choose what to do and say from the given prompts. Although, there is an overall storyline. Certain events are meant to happen in our lives. There are certain people we are meant to meet, certain passions we have been given, and certain feelings we are meant to experience. No matter what choice we make, the storyline will continue. Aspects of our storyline may change as we select prompts. Overall, the storyline will remain the same. Think of it as a straight path from A to B. We can either stay on the path or wander around the forest. We could also equate this wandering to the bends of a river.

Ultimately, you will still reach the ocean. You will still end up where you are meant to go. You may wander off for a while, but you are usually steered back to where you are meant to be. I say "usually," because we do have free will. We have prompts, but we decide what to do. What prompt we select influences the next set of prompts we get. We can carve a new path if we would like. I believe the path we are meant to follow will always be the most fulfilling, for it is the one the Divine Source planned with us.

Let's now dive into how the Divine Source keeps us on our paths. We have specific people we meet in our lives who provide us with the information we need to continue along our paths. Let's say you run into someone at the market who tells you something interesting that you decide to investigate when you get home. At home, you find that you are passionate about this and decide you will explore this further. You reach out to your newfound friend who delivered the information. Now, you are friends with this person and have found more things in common. You find more things you are interested in. Where did this person come from? Have they lived by you for your entire life? Did they just move here? How is it that you both decided to go to the market at the same time? Whatever the reason, you just met your best friend. Was this just a chance meeting? Sure, we could call it that. Let's mention some other coincidences that spur you in the direction you are meant to go in. The barista at your local coffee shop tells you about an upcoming event, and then you get to decide whether to go to the event or not. This is a new option being provided to you. Your mom tells you her friend has a job opening and wants to know if you are interested. Here is a new opportunity being provided to you. When you see an ad on your phone, you have the option to click on the ad to learn more. Everything I have just stated is a choice that fills some of your time here on Earth. You choose how to fill your time. However, there will always be something to do. Sometimes, we must search for something to do; other times, the opportunities come to us. Either way, we have a choice to do what we want to do. Why is it that we have all these options and opportunities in our lives? Why must we always have something to fill our time? Who provides this for us? Who gives us the thought to do this?

The source some of us call God has placed people, ads, information, and many other things in precarious ways for us to experience. All of which lead us down the best path for us to follow. A bird flew by at the perfect time to make me look up from my book and allow me to make eye contact with the pretty girl walking by in the park. Was this a coincidence? Or was this bird supposed to fly that exact path at that exact time to make me look up to make eye contact with her? What I know now is, I have a choice to make. Do I go talk to her, or do I keep reading this amazing book about how to fix the reality we created? Go talk to her. Interact with the girl who could be your soulmate. Who knows, she could even be your best friend. Funny thing is, if the bird had not flown by, you never would have had these thoughts. There are so many things happening in life people pass off as coincidence. Personally, I believe there are no coincidences. Absolutely everything happens for a reason.

Going back to the analogy of us being computers and we have screens that show us what we see, let's now look at how the internet shows us what we need to see, decided by who is in charge. There is an algorithm for every aspect of the internet. That algorithm will show you something that leads you somewhere else. Each of us has our own algorithm. If I went to Google on my phone and you went to Google on your phone, we would have different ads pop up. These ads have come up due to the decisions we have made while online. The only difference between our online presence and life presence is who is in charge. Online, the people in power have control over what you see. Yes, you made the decisions to create what has popped up next. However, you made the decisions based on what they created. Let's now look at reality. We have made decisions that created our reality within something created by a higher power. In both situations, the one in power has selected certain things to pop up to lead you in a certain way. Some people choose to follow the script, while others create their own. In our case, there are multiple scripts to follow, all of which have been created by God. It does not matter which script you follow or if you even stay on script. You are here to experience. You will come across so many choices within this experience: where you want to live, who you want to be friends with, what foods you eat, where you work, the topics of conversation, the possibilities are endless. However, certain things in life happen whether we want them to or not. As I said in the previous passage, there are no coincidences.

Some events happen in our lives that I believe to be unavoidable parts of our scripts. What I have mentioned is only a fraction of what could be unavoidable events. We could also go into illness and ailments. Some things are meant to happen to shape our souls for the greater good. They help shape the reality we create. This would explain my belief in co-creation. God is who we would be co-creating with, however, there are other beings Source has created. These beings create their realities. The beings you come into contact with help to shape your reality, as you help to create theirs. I believe they have been placed in your reality and you have been placed in theirs. Now, let's get into how we can interact with the Divine Source to better co-create. We can tell the Divine Source what we prefer to experience. When I do this, I always end the request with "if not this, then something better, as I know you have the best plan for me." For example, "thank you God for providing a way for me to buy this house. If not this house, then another house that is better suited for me, for I know you have the best plan for me." This does not mean you will be getting a house just because you asked for one. You must do your part to create reality as well. You must figure out how you will pay for this house or build this house. Then, your body will act upon the plan you have formulated with your thoughts. Perhaps you are already at a point of being able to afford the house, then, someone comes in with a cash offer of $20k over the asking price. You can choose to be in a bidding war or move on to find a new house. This person would be divine intervention, saying you are not meant to live here, keep looking. You have the choice to listen; as buying this house would alter the script. As I mentioned earlier, you can also carve your own path. In this belief system, the smart choice would be to keep looking, knowing that something better will come along.

In some scripts, people have negative thoughts that reoccur in their minds. Thoughts that may include causing harm to others. Why do they have these thoughts? I think there are forces of light and dark at play. Each side works to help or harm by swaying the minds of the people on the planet. Those of us conscious enough to decipher between the thoughts can make better decisions. However, some people have not attained this awareness of consciousness, so, they manifest both good and bad. I believe that everything is inherently good in all planes; that negativity is an illusion we see when we feel separate from God. We are one with God. The result of believing in the illusion of separateness has caused many things that we may no longer need to go through. We have free will and we create reality. We can create whatever we want. While feeling separate from God, we can experience fear. When we are fearful, we can believe in negative things. With this belief, we create negative entities that are also part of the illusion. We do not understand that we can change it. Had we changed it from the beginning, we would not go through negative thought processes. Now, some of us are here, having both positive and negative thoughts. I like to view them as love-based or fear-based. We have a choice of which thoughts to focus on. We can choose love or fear — positive or negative. Where our focus goes, energy flows. The only time an illusion can harm us is if we believe it can. If someone around you has stronger beliefs in a negative entity's ability to harm you than your confidence in the fact that you are safe, you can be harmed. Strengthening your understanding that everything that comes from fear-based thoughts is illusory you know you are safe. Sharing what you know is real and helping others to awaken from the illusion will liberate them from the hell they have created. Those of us with strong minds can lead the way for others to see past the illusions. We can create a better existence for all. It all starts with us taking the steps to show others that there is a better way, and us already seeing reality in a better way.

Some people have encountered negative entities. These experiences have a wide range of possibilities. However, these possibilities are within the collective's understanding of what negative entities are. What is the collective's understanding of a negative entity? Most people have only seen a negative entity in a scary movie, or a ghost hunting show. I think it is safe to say the only understanding of negative entities most people have is man-made. TV created a fear of these entities, and in the process, gave them power. I have released my previous understanding of negative entities and now have dominion over them. God has given everyone dominion over all things, all we have to do is accept it. With a deeper understanding of how to handle these beings, I have removed two of them from this physical plane. They were attached to homes and people I knew, but I helped them to rewire their brains and understand that they were the ones with the power to create. The entities were gone immediately. For me to come to this ability to handle entities, I had them in my dreams for quite some time. I was able to remove them once I found a mantra that allowed me to see the truth: "I see the truth, I see through illusion." This mantra focused my vision on what was true, seeing right through illusions. I gained confidence in my feeling of being with God as the truth was created, and the illusory entities dissipated, never to be seen again. To help my friends rewire their brains, I helped them to recognize what they had created and how it was created. Our thoughts create reality, our thoughts can create a demon. Removing thoughts surrounding demons removes the demon. This is not done by focusing on the removal. You place your focus on your eternal safety and give gratitude for the safe space you reside in. Keeping your focus on a safe reality, you create it.

There are a couple of "shields" I like to use to remember I am safe. Say the words, "God's light shines on me, and I am safe," or visualize a bubble around yourself and say, "the bubble around me allows only positive energy to come into me." Say them as often as you would like, especially before meditation. You are reaching higher states of consciousness and it is best to know you are safe. Another thing I do is clear or transmute energy throughout the day. My favorite prayer to think or say is, "I transmute all energy into love, joy and truth." All thoughts are prayers, and every prayer is answered. You can use any wording you wish to use to shield yourself or transmute energy, it is best to keep them loving, joyful, and truthful. Ensure you use positive words, as every word counts. Focus on what you are doing, not what you are preventing. Where your focus goes, energy flows.

Chapter 3
A Spiritual Perspective

An understanding of a spiritual plane is helpful to understand why certain things just happen. Knowing we are spiritual beings living a human experience, we know this experience is temporary. Eventually, we leave a material body and go somewhere else. I mentioned before that we are souls. Our souls are individual aspects of Spirit that wish to experience. Each soul has certain things it experiences. There is a co-creation between our soul in a spiritual plane and our soul incarnate. The soul in a spiritual plane has certain things it wants to experience, creating plot points for the soul incarnate to experience. The rest of life experience is the free will of the soul incarnate. Remembering that our soul is one aspect of Spirit, this experience is a co-creation with God. These experiences are plentiful. We have had and will have many more. Having a belief in reincarnation helps to understand eternal existence. The thought of being able to have experiences while not residing in a body opens the door to understanding that we chose certain things to happen before living a life, and that we chose to be here. This is one way of thinking that allows one to perceive all of life as an experience of God.

Earlier in the book, I mentioned all that exists is God. By enhancing our understanding of what this means, we see God in everything. The ground we walk on is God, the air we breathe is God, the TV on the wall is God, I am God, you are God, we are all God. This is one material portion of heaven, one way of experience in the infinite possible ways of experience. We can create whatever we want. God experiences everything He wants to experience from all He knows. Likewise, we can create our lives in any way we want to. However, we must acknowledge the fact that bad things have happened. Why would God want to experience this? Those souls get to experience another aspect of what we know. All of creation is for expansion, experience, growth, and perspective. The perspectives of the bad allow us to see the good more easily. How do we know skinny without fat? It takes both to understand which one we want to experience. Thankfully, we are souls that experience these events. What happens here in this material plane does not continue throughout eternity. Our souls have learned the difference between good and bad. The only time we will experience lifetimes with "bad" is if we choose to. The soul gets to pick what to experience, just like we pick movies on Netflix. Some people love watching horror movies. Some people enjoy romantic comedies. With this perspective of a spiritual plane, we select certain plot points of the movie and give the characters free will, then, you erase your memory as you jump into the movie. At least, that is how some of us have decided to experience this life. The option to remember our past lives or life experience in a spiritual plane is an option we can select before incarnating. Some people in our reality do, but many of us do not. It is all for the sake of experience. Picking certain plot points in the movie is how I explain some of the random happenings in life, some of which would not be considered desirable choices in this collective reality; for instance, things such as being paralyzed, blind, born without limbs, tortured, and many other experiences that we have deemed as bad. Thankfully, all plot points are inherently good and what we have deemed as bad is only experienced by some souls. All of these experiences change the way an individual perceives reality. There are infinite possibilities within what God wants to experience. All have been and are being explored.

With infinite possibilities, we have an infinite amount of time. Time exists as a learning tool for how to effectively spend eternity, and to provide a different perspective. Time is only present in some realities; realities such as the one you reside in. Time is given its meaning with the words we attach meaning to. In our totality, which is Spirit, time is nonexistent. All possible experiences happen simultaneously. Realities with time provide different ways for us to experience. With this understanding, we realize we have chosen to be here, experiencing this moment. We have chosen to watch this movie. We have chosen some of the characters in the movie. We have written some parts of the script. And we are here for expansion, experience, growth, and perspective. "We," being the souls that we are. The body we inhabit is just a vehicle for us to operate in this reality. Like a character in a video game, sometimes, we build the character and choose the details such as the body shape, color, hairstyle, eye color, and so on and so forth. Other times, we select at random, seeing that it is just a body/vessel, and we can relive this life in another way if we wish.

Reincarnation is the process of picking another movie. You can even pick the same movie. Almost everyone has experienced déjà vu. Most of the time, when we experience deja vu, it is that our imagination has created the event because we want to experience deja vu. However, there is a reason we experience it and are talking about it now. It helps us to understand that we have lived this life before, and it makes us ask ourselves questions. Some experiences of deja vu could include seeing something you have already seen before, even though you have never been there, seeing an event playout exactly as you had seen in a vision, and not being able to recall if it was a dream or something you saw before this life, or even knowing the feelings of certain places before you get there. Regardless of the way in which you have experienced deja vu, you understand you have been here before. This should bring you comfort. This is a simulation you can restart after this life. We experience deja vu until we make decisions we have never made in our previous playthroughs of this life; decisions that would alter the trajectory of this life, such as becoming a musician rather than being a doctor — although, you may have already done that. We can create any life we want from where we are now. We get to decide where to go. We are responsible for what we create. This is what we get to do throughout all of existence. This temporary experience is just one aspect of it. We can do whatever we want in this movie and select another movie if we want.

Before anyone asks about suicide, I will give my understanding of it here. In the previous chapter, I stated that we can restart after this life. Yes, suicide would put you into another life. However, the soul dictates what to experience. You may very well go through the exact life again, so, why put yourself through the same experiences again? Learn the lessons you came here to learn and move on. You get to be here to create the life you want to experience. Have trust that you already are experiencing the life you came here to live, and you will watch it fall into place for you.

Having an understanding that we are souls and there are other planes of existence, we can understand that heaven is described in many ways because of so many different perspectives. Yes, we can go to a floating cloud city where the streets are paved with gold. We can also relive lives on Earth or other planets. There are so many different ways to experience life, and we experience all of them. We are always in heaven; view this life as a glorious experience you get to have. Love that you get to be here. Every aspect of life is enjoyable with the right perspective. We watch sad movies, and we also watch happy movies; we watch all sorts of movies to bring out different emotions. This life is full of emotions we get to experience. It is why we are here. Experience the life you came here to live and love every minute of it. You create what you experience, create your ideal life.

Chapter 4
How to Better Co-Create Reality with the Divine Source

In chapter 2, we talked about telling God what we would prefer to experience. This is one way we can better co-create reality with the Divine Source. There are many ways, and I will cover some of them here. This is not to say these are the only ways, or these are the right ways, but these are the ways that have proven to work for me. If what I have done resonates with you, feel free to use the information in co-creating your reality.

"Do to others what you want them to do to you." This is something many of us have heard growing up. Everything we say, do, and even think is reflected back to us. View the external world as a mirror for your inner world. Everything going on around you is what you have created with your thoughts, words, and actions. You put all of this into the world, you are now experiencing it. Whether it was the thoughts you had last week, the ones you are having now, or thoughts you had 5 years ago, they manifested in some way into your reality. As we grow and heal through these events, our inner world reflects to the outer world the areas we can work on. This could be our thought processes of others, our confidence in ourselves, dissipating anxiety, any number of things. Whether it is this body you reside in experiencing it, or another body you see going through something. You are seeing it for a reason. You have the opportunity to grow as you interpret the world around you. Seeing the world as your mirror allows one to realize oneness. Seeing one person going through anxiety as a part of oneself shows you that you experience anxiety in some way. There is an aspect of yourself to heal. Seeing someone who lacks confidence shows you that you lack confidence in some way. These experiences show you what aspects of yourself to work on. The words you hear others speak may very well be a reflection of your thoughts, as our thoughts become our words.

The thoughts you have of yourself create possible thought processes for others. Thoughts of others create possibilities for them to think that of others — possibly you. These thoughts are not necessarily reflected by the same person you think of. They can be reflected in any way God sees fit so that you become aware of what you are creating. It is important to remember that anything you think someone else is thinking is an assumption. If you are going to make assumptions, make sure they are love-based. If you are someone who has negative thoughts, let's make an affirmative prayer together, and then look at some ways to change this. "I am grateful that I see things through God's eyes. Thank you, God, for allowing me to see all areas in my life in which I can grow. It has been so transformative to see the aspects of myself I wished to change. Those aspects were lower vibrational habits. Having changed them into higher vibrational habits, I am now a much more joyful and loving person. I have created a reality in which all things work for me. I choose to see myself and others in our highest light. I am grateful for the awareness to see the transformation within and around myself. Thank you, God, amen." The first part of this affirmative prayer is something I say every day: "I am open to seeing things your way Father. I am grateful to see things through God's eyes."

Affirmative prayer is one way of changing aspects of yourself that no longer serve you. I picture every second of my life as a blank canvas. I get to choose what to paint and choose which aspects to create an image. With a blank canvas, there are no past paintings to block my view. I am free to create myself, as I am not defined by my past. I am free. I create myself everyday with affirmative prayers, openness to hear God, and being of service to the best of my abilities. The affirmative prayers can change from time to time, as we are all ever-evolving beings of love and light.

Another way is awareness. Without awareness, you do not know what to change. With the affirmative prayer we just made, you will become aware of the negative aspects of yourself. This will allow you to "think again." Instead of spending time fixing the issue, say this, "I transmute all energy into love, joy, and truth." Then, positively think about anything else. You have removed the thoughts of negativity and replaced them with positivity, thus creating a more positive reality for you to experience. You can come up with any phrase you like, or you can use the one I provided you. The main aim here is becoming aware. Believe that you already are, and so it will be.

Asking yourself questions such as, "is my thought love-based or fear-based?" throughout the day will keep you in a state of awareness. There are no neutral thoughts, and this question can bring to light many aspects of yourself you may want to change. Again, it takes awareness to ask the question. Set a reminder on your phone for once an hour, once every 15 minutes, as often as you would like. Name the reminder "Love or Fear?" This is an easy way to keep yourself awake throughout the day.

A very important part of co-creation is having a healthy diet. Diet is a major factor in bettering our ability to co-create. Look into blood-type dieting. Our bodies are different and not everyone is meant to be entirely plant based. Knowing your blood type and changing your diet to fit you will increase your connection with source. View your body as a vehicle. Some vehicles need gasoline, some of them need diesel. Whatever source of fuel your vehicle needs, you use it. Do the same for your body. Your body is your temple. The better the foundation your temple has, the easier it is to communicate with source.

Alongside proper diet, I began exercising, doing yoga, listening to positive affirmations, and talking to people with friendlier personalities. What helped the most was being conscious of what I allowed to come into my reality; what I watched and what I listened to. Every word we hear and speak is important. It builds the reality we live in. It affects the prompts we get to choose from. I noticed the music I listened to was speaking repetitive negativity into my life. The emotions I felt when I watched a depressing movie brought more depression into my life. I was inputting negative energy into my reality. I think of it as plugging a USB drive into the computer I am and uploading negative information into my computer. This caused the computer to produce more negative images. I figured the best way to stop this was to change what I input into my reality. I became conscious of what I watch and listen to. I made sure everything I was inputting into my reality was positive. I began noticing positive changes in my reality. Every day, things I would become upset over were no longer an issue for me. I was able to notice this change in myself. The changes I made brought more joy into my life. I began to find more ways to make myself a happier person. I began meditating. This is the most important part of becoming closer to the Divine Source. Creating a relationship with God. In order to better co-create reality with God, you must learn how to listen. Anyone can pray, but who can listen?

Incorporating these changes into your life builds a proper foundation that allows you to better communicate with the Divine Source. Not to say you cannot do this without these steps, although they make it easier. Now, we can get into what I believe to be the fun stuff. There are many ways of communicating with our creator and the creations who are here to help us. One way is through meditation and prayer. Meditation allows one to find stillness, in the stillness one can hear their inner guidance. Prayer is every thought we have, every word we speak, and every action we choose to make. Praying with intention tells God the direction we would like to go. Aside from prayer and meditation, there are many ways of divination. We can also call these mediums. Mediums can be cocoa leaves, books, tarot cards, people... really, anything can be a medium. People use all sorts of mediums to connect themselves with Spirit. The ones I am most familiar with are numerology, clairaudience, and tarot. Numerology is the study of the meaning behind numbers. I like to call them angel numbers. Angels are always around us, giving some of us messages through numbers as they are ever present in our lives. A license plate you see has 222 on it. Perhaps you wake up at a certain time every day, the clock shows 11:11 when you look at it, and/or your receipts have repeating numbers. There are numbers everywhere in our lives and if we pay attention, we can see the patterns. The numbers that are messages do not have to be repeated to be a message; for instance, one message I have been getting frequently is 347. This is a message of congratulations; it tells me the angels wish for me to continue along my current path. This is one of many interpretations of the numbers. This is where you use your intuition to discern between interpretations or come up with your own. What resonates with you? Does this interpretation feel right to you?

Numbers could come from anywhere. They could be single digits or many digits, arranged in any order. Using your intuition you will know if the sign is meant for you. You should get a good feeling inside when you see the number repeatedly. If you continue to see the number throughout your life, it means that the angels really want you to see this specific message. If you wish to find interpretations for the numbers you come across in your reality, google "xxx angel number." "xxx" signifies the numbers you should insert. When I first started finding interpretations, I would click a different site each time I saw the number. I figured I was sent the number again due to my inability to properly interpret the message. Now, I receive the message on the first attempt. I also encourage you to research your life path and destiny number. You can find a calculator for these numbers on Google. Type in "life path number calculator," and there will be several sites that come up to help you find this number. I would have written about them here if they were not another book worth of information. Personally, I find them to be quite fascinating. They also help you to see interpretations of single-digit numbers. They will further your understanding of angel numbers with multiple digits. Eventually, you will be able to interpret messages without having to ask Google. It is similar to learning a language. This language is communicating with beings we cannot see — well, most of us anyway. As I mentioned earlier, there are many ways these other beings contact us. There are different mediums, and there are different signs from angels. They can be anything. It is your reality you have created. Angels and other beings will use what you know to communicate with you.

Another medium is tarot. Tarot readings have been around for a very long time. The oldest complete deck that is known dates back to the 1400s. These cards have no meaning other than the meanings we have given them. We could read a deck of playing cards if we gave each card a meaning. The way I know the cards to work is through the intention. I clear my mind and focus my thoughts on the intention of the reading. I describe to God what spread I will use, and I ask the question over and over in my mind as I shuffle the cards. I continue shuffling until I am prompted to stop. Then, I deal the cards in the aforementioned spread. The images and meanings I have attributed to the cards help me to better understand the messages that God has for me, or messages for me to give to another. Some people claim to predict the future with these cards; however, the future is a possibility. Yes, we can look at possible futures with the cards, but the truth is, we create reality with infinite variability.

Earlier in this chapter, I mentioned the term clairaudience. Most people have heard the term clairvoyance — the ability to have prophetic dreams, seeing souls, and having visions during the waking hours. Clairvoyance is not limited to this, but those are some of the aspects. Clairaudience is the ability to hear other beings most cannot see. Most people who have this gift of hearing voices get called crazy, delusional, or schizophrenic, thus making it quite difficult for one to talk about hearing spirits or angels. For me, my clairaudience comes in the form of a thought. I have learned to tell the difference between my thoughts and the thoughts that are a higher or lower vibrational being communicating with me. They have different tones of voice, just like each of us speak in different ways. I can hear different beings inside my thoughts. This is telepathy from them being around me and communicating with me. This way, I can act as a medium to the spirit world. I act as a medium for myself and others, delivering messages I am meant to deliver. Whether or not the receiver is ready for the message or if I am ready to deliver the message, I must do, say, or in some cases, write, whatever it is they tell me. Perhaps I am on to something. No one knows for certain what is going on here. Although many masters throughout time have said we are the ones who create it.

Since you have read this far into the book, you must have found ways to heal yourself. You have the choice to heal yourself or ignore the message. It is your reality, your choice. Pray to Source, and any being of love and light to assist you. These beings are always with you and willing to assist. Just ask. During your healing, especially after your healing, you will have a much better understanding of how to co-create reality with Source. Many of us call this raising our vibration. As we heal ourselves and change our habits to higher vibrational habits, we raise our vibrational frequency.

Here is a list of ways in which we can raise our vibration:

1. Living with an attitude of gratitude. Be thankful for everything you already have in life. Be thankful for everything you get to experience. Be thankful for your body. Be thankful for the parts of your body you like and dislike.

2. Be happy with everything you get to experience.

3. Spend time in nature. For instance, walk barefoot on the Earth.

4. Spend time with animals, pet them regularly.

5. Meditate. Take an Epsom salt bath. Lay in the tub meditating.

6. Create a safe space for yourself; a sanctuary where you can be your true self.

7. Develop a spiritual practice that aligns with your moral code.

8. Exercise.

9. Eat healthy food.

10. Drink lots of water.

11. Pray.

12. Tell people they are beautiful. If you think someone's outfit is cute, then tell them; help them feel good about themselves.

13. Occasionally disconnect from technology.

14. Say no to things you do not feel like doing. There are certain things in life that you must do, if such thing is toxic and/or draining you, say no. Instead, do what you want to in life.

15. Breathe deeply and practice mindfulness. Mindfulness is the practice of realizing where you are and being thankful for it. It also includes being thankful for the people in your space that you get to interact with; being mindful of their thoughts and feelings while still speaking your truth.

16. Read positive material.

17. Listen to positive music.

18. Write, speak, or listen to positive affirmations.

19. Hug someone.

20. Organize your living space.

21. Surround yourself with positive people. Remove negative people that refuse to change from your life. They are at a point in their lives where they must go through these negative emotions and feelings, and you are now beyond this.

22. Smile all the time.

23. Watch a comedy and laugh. Truly laugh and let yourself be happy.

24. Let go of the need to control everything. Be optimistic. Focus on abundance. Trust that there is enough for everyone. There is no need to feel you are lacking anything. Lighten up about everything, life always goes on. No matter what, life goes on. The thoughts you are having about what happened last week - the one you think will ruin your life - forget about it. How many of those have you had? Were you happy a month later? Were you thinking about it still? Maybe. Maybe not. Does not matter, your life went on and you had other things to do. Replace fear with love. Your life has always continued. Look where you are now. Be happy.

25. Sleep when you are tired.

26. Get outside your comfort zone.

27. Reduce added sugar intake, as well as alcohol and drug usage. Completely cut it out when you can if you have not already.

28. Be more generous with your love, especially to yourself. Loving yourself is the key to loving others. Look in the mirror and say, "hey beautiful, I love you. You are doing amazing things, carry on."

29. Do nice things for people without any expectation of reciprocation.

30. Avoid complaining. Where you focus your energy is what you attract. Complaining only attracts more of what you complain about.

31. Have meaningful conversations with others.

32. Get a massage. Try Reiki healing.

33. Set an intention for each day.

34. Volunteer your time in spaces/places where you feel you can be of great benefit to others.

35. Forgive everyone, especially yourself. Everyone has made mistakes in their life. It is what you choose to do afterwards that determines who you decide to be. Do not blame others for anything. Remember you create your reality, not them. If it is your fault, forgive yourself for making a mistake; if it is someone else's, assure them that everything will be okay. Inspire them in some way, shape, or

form. After all, we are here to love one another and lift each other up. We should spread as much love as we can. You will always move forward if you are always doing the next right thing.

The list is more of a to-do list than a set of instructions on how to better co-create reality. It is your decision to do them. We are building a strong foundation to co-create reality. My way is one of many, and it will speed up your process. Once you have created this positive foundation, you now see the things you were doing wrong. Only you can fix them. I will get into the things many of us are doing wrong in the next chapter, and I will do my best to keep it brief. Not many of us enjoy being lectured on what we are doing wrong. However, I will also tell you how to prevent yourself from repeating these mistakes.

Back to how to better co-create reality with the Divine Source. Now that we have a positive foundation, including ways to communicate with our Source, the next logical step is to begin communicating with Source, especially listening. Remember God and His or Her created beings are here to help us. These beings are much more knowledgeable than we are. They know what is best for us in any given situation, and we have the choice to listen. One way to start is by asking God for an answer in a tough situation. Instead of asking other people, go within to ask yourself. If you are meant to know the answer, the answer will come to you. This leads me to question if you are meant to go down the path you are following. If God is not giving you answers to help you proceed along your current path, then perhaps you are not meant to follow through with it. This would indicate that it is time to ask God where you should go next. Also, ask God how to get there. Pray for assistance in reaching this new path. Pray for assistance in acquiring all that is needed along said path to reach your goals. Give gratitude for the assistance you have received in this transitional period. This is how we communicate with our thoughts, words, and ears. How can we better co-create with our feelings? We must do this on a subconscious level. This is where listening to positive affirmations comes to play. When listening to positive affirmations such as, "I am beautiful, I am happy, I am living in abundance," and so on and so forth, they make you feel better. The feeling you get when someone tells you they like your hair or they like your shoes makes you feel good. That feeling of happiness can be held throughout your day. Likewise, listening to positive affirmations instead of music for a week would generate a much happier subconscious feeling. Music can also make you happy, depending on the lyrics. Now, how does this feeling help you co-create reality? This brings me back to the law of attraction. We attract what we feel. If I feel happy, I attract happy experiences. If I feel I am rich, I attract financial abundance into my physical reality. This can happen overnight. To continue this flow of abundance, you must continue feeling this way. If you get pulled down out of feeling happy, ask yourself, "what is going on in my life that stops me from smiling? Why am I not happy right now? What can I do to change this?" Remember, you create your reality. You brought in the negative energy that has made you unhappy, so you must remove it. Perhaps it was an unavoidable part of your script, an obstacle you were meant to overcome.

Affirmations play a very important role in creating our reality. However, focus on the desired reaction as you use affirmations. If your desired reaction is abundance, ask yourself what type of abundance you are looking for. Get specific and know that it is yours. You are worthy of anything you desire. If your desired reaction is happiness, "I am happy" will work, so long as you believe it. Be careful of what affirmations you say and remember what the reaction is. An affirmation such as, "I am resilient" creates events for you to be resilient. "I am strong" creates events you get to show your strength. Use affirmations to create the events you enjoy doing. You create this reality the way you want to experience it. Having a disciplined understanding of how your thoughts create reality allows you to know what you are creating, and in turn allows you to have control over the experiences you will have. Know that as you confess, you shall possess. You think your world into existence. You feel your world into existence. You speak and take actions that create this world. Every decision you make, including the emotions you choose to feel, translates to how you experience life. Use your words wisely. Focus on your thoughts and feelings. Know that you are in control and take responsibility.

I believe negative experiences are unnecessary for us to have during our lives. Obstacles can be positive. We choose whether or not to be happy. We choose how to perceive the occurrences of our lives. The only time we will have negative experiences is if we have negative thoughts. "All that we are arises from our thoughts." Negative experiences come from having negative thought processes, and as a result, we create negative obstacles. I choose to experience everything positively. This way, I only manifest positive experiences. It took time for me to find the light in each experience, as there are lessons to be learned from these processes. I found happiness in the amount of time it took for me to overcome these thoughts becoming shorter each time. Eventually, we rid ourselves completely of negative thoughts and emotions. Ask yourself if the thought process you are having is what you would like to be manifested into your life. If the answer is "no," remove the thought process. If the answer is "yes," manifest away, you, beautiful reality creator.

Chapter 5
What Many of Us are Doing Wrong

Choosing our words carefully is important in reality creation. Every thought we think is creative, so we must choose them carefully as well. Using what you have learned in the previous chapters, this will become easier. In this chapter, I will go over what I have experienced myself as being "wrong," and how to prevent repeating mistakes.

When it comes to prayer, the way you pray is very important. For example, saying "please God, I ask that you heal my son," is affirming that your son is not healed. Instead of asking, thank God in advance. Say, "thank you, God, for healing my son." Thanking God in advance affirms to the Universe that you are currently in possession of what you have manifested, and that you are holding faith that God has done what you thanked Him for. This is the faith to move a mountain. Trusting and knowing God has already done what you thanked Him for.

Another one that I have experienced in churches is pastors telling people to ask for forgiveness. You have no reason to ask for forgiveness. By asking, you are telling God you have done wrong, and creating the feeling of having done wrong. In this particular case, you need not even thank God for forgiveness. You were never condemned. The only one who needs to forgive you is you. Instead, what you should do is thank God for the awareness and clarity he has bestowed upon you. Another example would be asking for money. Thank the Universe for bestowing wealth upon you. Expect that your prayer has been heard and answered. Asking God for money is creating the reality that you are not wealthy. Changing your mindset from asking to already being blessed with creates the feeling required for the law of attraction to work. Rather than ask, continue to thank God in advance. This creates the proper thought processes to keep you in the right state of mind. Please and thank you go a long way. I thank God every day for everything I get to experience. God is the reason we get to experience life. I thank Him as well as his creations who help us daily. "God, please continue to provide everything we need in our daily lives. We are eternally grateful for all you provide for us. We are so thankful you allow us to live these lives how we see fit. Thank you for allowing us to create the lives we wish to experience. We are worthy of anything we want to experience thanks to you. We love you Father, namaste. Amen." Alongside these prayers, we must do the work. Whatever you pray for, you will be given thought prompts. Follow the prompts to realize your creation.

Aside from prayer, there are some other things I have noticed people have done "wrong." One thing is casting judgment on oneself and others. Do your best to understand that you do not know what is going on in their lives. You have very little idea as to why they do what they do, wear what they decide to wear, or why they look the way they do. Every person has a purpose, as do you. Each of us is different in some way. Find the good in everyone you see. See them in their highest light. See yourself in your highest light as well. By seeing the best in others and yourself, you manifest the best for all. Judging yourself or others takes your time away from the beautiful reality you are creating.

Understand that judgment is a fear-based thought process, and there are no neutral thoughts; there are only thoughts of love or fear. The key is becoming aware of your thought processes. Once you are aware of them, you can ask yourself if this is a love or fear-based thought. There are many ways to change perception. I am giving you a basic understanding of what happens in your mind, so you can come up with your way of doing things.

What is seeing ourselves and others in our highest light? The way I do it is to see them as loving, joyful, and honest expressions of us. Knowing that they are me and I am them, the thoughts I think of them I am thinking of myself. If I want others to see me as loving, joyful, wise, honest, compassionate, funny, successful, etc. Then, I affirm those things for them. I say "thank you for your blessings. I am grateful to share space with you. You are wise and I can learn from you. I enjoy being around your loving presence." These are thoughts I say to them in my head. Sometimes I tell the person what I affirm for them also. I frame it in a compliment they are willing to receive. Knowing what I put into the world comes back to me, I realize that if the other people here are also me, then I am giving to myself. As I see this wholeness, I experience peace and harmony.

When talking to other sentient beings, do your best to always spread positivity. If you realize that what you say may hurt someone else, do your best to change this behavior. You are likely to have done this to others. Once you are aware of the problem, you can change the behavior. By spreading positivity to others, you not only raise your vibration, but theirs as well. We are here to help one another. There is no reason to be negative towards others, as we have no idea what they are going through. However, we can always do our best to be a shining light of happiness in their lives. Also, never self-deprecate to make others feel better about themselves. For example, if someone comes to you saying, "I hate when I forget my phone in the other room." Agreeing with them, saying, "I do that all the time" would create the reality that you do this all the time. Instead, say, "I suppose you will have to walk over there and get it." They stated what was wrong, you stated what to do. This creates a solution-finding mentality. Another example of self-deprecation can come when trying to be humble. Someone compliments your work, and you say, "It is not as good as so and so." In your attempt to boost someone else, you lower your view of yourself and create a comparison. What you should do is accept the compliment graciously, then, give the other person a compliment. You are worthy of recognition, and so are they. Be the amazing soul you are and enjoy the kind words from others.

Avoid the word "not" when praying, wishing, or setting intentions. The word "not" is associated with a negative feeling, commonly used to say, "I am not this." "This" is what you are bringing into your reality. You are also bringing it in with negativity. An example of this would be, "I am not fat." By saying "fat," you are bringing more fat into reality. By saying "not," you are speaking of it negatively. This will bring more negatives into your reality. One example is stress-eating, which leads to more fat. Another example would be "I will not talk badly about others." Think of this intention as saying, "I will talk badly about others." Instead say, "I will always speak positively about others." Rather than trying to fix your mistakes, build a better future. Speaking in this manner focuses on creating a more positive future rather than changing a negative past. As Socrates said, "The secret to change is to focus all of your energy, not on fighting the old, but on building the new." I realize he said "not" in this quote. However, he was laying emphasis on the fact that he is aware that it is better to focus your attention on where you want to go rather than change where you have been.

The words "but," "want," and "need," should also be avoided. "But" is usually followed by an excuse, although it is sometimes used to provide an alternate viewpoint in conversation. There are better words to use, such as "however," "although," and "on the other hand." The words "want" and "need" both affirm that you currently do not have something. When you affirm that you do not have something, that is what you attract. For example, "I want more money" affirms that you lack funds. You create your reality in a position of lack instead of a position of abundance. Instead of using the words "want" or "need," feel as though you already have what you need. Give thanks to God for the blessing he has bestowed upon you. Thanking God in advance is a wonderful way to manifest from a place of abundance. In the case of money, tithing is a wonderful practice to manifest wealth. Giving is the ultimate sign of having received. The more I have, the more I can give. "Tithe" is 10 percent. Giving 10 percent of your income ensures a steady supply of financial abundance. The way I started was by creating a budget. The money left after paying bills is the amount that I would take 10 percent from. If I had an extra $200 a month, I would give $20 in some way. Some months, I gave more; others, I gave less. I always give when I am prompted to do so. Another way we use "want" and "need" is with materials, "I need a screwdriver." By removing this phrase and replacing it with "I will get this" or "can you get this for me?" you create thought processes of already having what is needed.

Manifestation comes from every single thought we have. Removing "needs" and "wants" will allow you to come to an acceptance that you have everything you need. Have full faith that all of your needs are met daily. God provides everything you believe if you wholly believe it.

Holding faith that your needs are met can be easy. It becomes especially easy when we stop entertaining negative stories in our minds. Worrying about tomorrow takes away strength from today. Rather than placing your focus on what could go wrong, place your focus on what could go right. By doing this, you open your mind to all the possibilities of the situation at hand; possibilities you would not have seen if you had focused your energy on worrying. Remember, where focus goes, energy flows. When you worry, you create a reality with a negative ending to the situation you are thinking about. When you focus on what could go right, you are creating a reality with a positive ending. What would you like to manifest? A negative ending, or a positive one? Yes, you should be aware that negative outcomes are possible. By not focusing on negative outcomes, you are showing God that you trust all will be well. You believe the best will come. Stay optimistic. If anything goes wrong, you will overcome whatever happens. You always do. After all, that is why you are still alive and can sit down to read a book today.

Chapter 6
How to Break Self-Imposed Limitations

What do I mean when I say self-imposed limitations? I mean limitations we have placed on ourselves, whether they are from us or others. When we decide to believe in them, they are self-imposed limitations. When someone says, "You cannot do that, it is impossible," you might believe them and stop trying. This was not the case for Elon Musk. He has done the impossible many times now. As I mentioned earlier in the book, the man is landing rockets back on Earth after sending them to space. You may think of that as an extreme example, so, let's look at self-limitations some of us may set daily. Some of us may think we are not good enough to do certain things. We could say things like, "I suck at math and will fail this test." This limits your ability to learn math. It also creates the reality where you do fail the test. After this test, you may or may not learn to study harder to understand the material. Some of us must work harder on certain subjects, while some of us have it easy, the knowledge just comes to us. While one student believes in their ability to solve math problems, the other doubts their ability to solve math problems. Both are creating their reality. Another example is, "I cannot do this; it is too difficult." The task may require effort, and not necessarily be difficult. You can say it is easy. You could say it is easy to start your own business. Tell yourself you have all the support you need to get the job done. That all is well. Rather than focusing on the risks, focus on how to overcome the challenges so that you can be successful. Visualize yourself already being a successful business owner. Place your focus on optimistic outcomes. Good things will come to you. We can do absolutely anything we set our minds to. All we have to do is keep our thoughts in the same place optimistically. Of course, some things are out of our control. I gave my reasons for these earlier in the book. Know that God has something better in store for you.

The lessons you learn from a shortcoming always have a purpose.

We have unlimited potential. All we must do is believe in ourselves. We can do anything. Some people run over 25 miles in a day. My aunt is one of these people. She runs almost every day. She loves to run. She set her mind to it. Now, she is accomplishing her goal. I am very impressed with how far she can run. "I could not run that far," would be a self-imposed limitation I could my place on myself. I am positive that with time and proper training, one day I could run that far. We could also take this from a reading standpoint. Some people read one to five books a day. The self-imposed limitation here would be, "I could never read an entire book in a day." The truth is, you certainly could, depending on the size of the book. Also, the people who read books all the time are more likely to read an entire book in a day. Remember, this is your reality, you have your likes and dislikes. This does not mean you cannot do what you dislike; rather, it means you would prefer to spend your time doing what you like. As you should, life is much more enjoyable this way. Fill your time with things you enjoy doing, especially what you do for work.

Another self-limiting phrase is "this is too hard." Whatever the task at hand may be, it is only hard if you think it is. "I could never work through my anxiety, depression, fear and paranoia; it is just too difficult. I do not know what to do." You are limiting yourself. You do know what to do, go get help. Therapy is a wonderful way to help you overcome these aspects of yourself, by speaking about what has hurt you and venting it out. However, you must be willing to go through the pain of the events that caused these problems for you. You must experience the root cause of the problem. Handling this takes away the problems you created after the cause. You can take on the problems alone. However, it is helpful to have an outside perspective of what is going on. You can heal however fast you are willing to go. For the negative emotions listed above, think of them as products of blockages. These blockages cause buildup. Buildup would be negative thoughts, emotions, feelings, words, and actions. To remove the blockage, you must forgive the person who hurt you. This person may even be you. You may have cast judgment upon yourself for something you have done. You are living a human experience; you are bound to have made mistakes. Forgiveness is for the liberation of the forgiver. The forgiver liberates themselves from the negative thought processes they had once put themselves through by removing the blockage.

So, how do we break these limitations? First, you must become aware that you are setting them. Become conscious of the words you speak. As you confess, you shall possess. Be conscious of the effect these words have on creating your reality. Every word counts. Every thought counts. Thoughts become words, and words become actions. We have a choice to set limitations on ourselves or to be free. With pre-existing limitations, it is quite easy to remove them. You create your reality. Simply say, "I remove all limitations I once placed on myself. I remove all limitations others previously placed on me." Then, you believe this to be true. Go another step further, replace the limitations you just deleted with belief in yourself with words like, "I can do anything I set my mind to. I am a being of unlimited potential. I have everything needed to accomplish my biggest dreams." These are called positive affirmations. The more positive thoughts and intentions you have, the more positive you become. The step of deleting them may not even be necessary for you. It made me feel better at first, but I realized I was still focusing on the negative by deleting something. Here is where "I transmute all energy into love, joy, and truth," can be useful again. Then, positive affirmations.

This was a rather short chapter, but an important one. After deleting your limitations, you could still create more. Remain aware of the thoughts occurring in your mind. You can choose to have them or to think about something else. Your thoughts influence what you do. When you realize you are in a negative thought process, ask yourself, "what is the reason I am thinking negatively? What part of myself do I need to heal?" Whatever the answer is, heal it and move on. Find your happy place. We must vent sometimes. However, we can heal many of our problems if we stop talking about them. Complaining only attracts more of said problems. We should focus on the good parts of our lives. Tell people about this awesome book that has helped you heal parts of yourself. It is cool to read. Tell people about the amazing hike you had. Tell people about the interesting dream you had. Tell the world whatever it is you are excited about. Talk about the good, and eventually, good is all there will be. When you believe you are healed, you know you are whole. If a negative thought process comes up, transmute it, and think again. Eventually, good really is all there is in your mind. Everything else that happens is up to fate. In this state of wholeness, the obstacles that do arise are much easier to handle. Send them your love and gratitude, and you will then see what is to be learned and how to integrate it into your reality with ease.

Chapter 7
How to Shift Realities

This is my interpretation of how our reality works in this collective consciousness, and how we can shift realities within this collective consciousness. Let's go back to the analogy of you being the computer. You choose what websites to view. You choose the realities to experience. You choose the people you talk to. You choose the job you work. You choose the country to live in. You have the power to choose the reality you wish to experience.

Shifting realities can be as simple as moving to another part of the world and leaving everything behind. Now, you are in a completely different area of the world, speaking a different language, practicing different customs, and having completely different conversations. To me, this would be a different reality, just like playing different video game. What types of jobs are over here? What kinds of foods are over here? What kind of activities can you do for fun? I presume they differ from where you were before. You have placed yourself into another reality by placing yourself in a different part of the world. Now, you are surrounded by many different types of people you have never seen before, with every single one of them creating their respective realities and adding to the collective reality of the region. Remember the net analogy from chapter 1? One part of the net with individual intersections creating realities may look different than a part of the net on the other side of the planet. However, we are all a part of the same net.

Knowing there are many realities within the reality all the sentient beings on earth collectively create, we can consciously travel between the realities. How do we shift out of the main reality? For this, we will refer to chapter 1 — the part where I talked about enlightenment and already living in heaven. To attain enlightenment, you must learn to vibrate in harmony with the ego and the id. The ego is your perceived reality. You would be shifting your consciousness into another reality; one where you can see the reality you reside in and also understand that this reality is created by every sentient being here at this moment of existence. Understanding reality changes over time, seeing how reality is created from the sponsoring thoughts of every sentient being here. Sponsoring thoughts are the ones we have accepted to be reality. All sponsoring thoughts everywhere create the collective reality. The reality was much different 100 years ago when there were different sentient beings here. It was different 1000 years ago, and so on and so forth. Reality is a construct of what everyone believes to be true. Reality is a "majority rules" affair. It depends on how many people believe in a certain direction. Another aspect of enlightenment is finding your purpose here, and then to live that purpose. A cab driver can be an enlightened being. Being enlightened does not mean you are a spiritual teacher. It simply means you are at peace in the body you reside in, serving your purpose as you have chosen to. The keyword from the previous sentence is "peace." The sense of peace that all is going exactly as it should be in your life, and not thinking about where you should be in life. You are happy with where you are, knowing that you get to listen and go with the flow. You know that all is provided as you continue along your journey.

Let's elaborate on sponsoring thoughts. Sponsoring thoughts contribute to the creation of reality. Many people believe money is the root of all evil. This would be a sponsoring thought. Any job where you feel you are doing good is now a low-paying job. A belief in good and bad is a sponsoring thought. We as humans have decided what is good and bad. Any belief made by any person or group of people is a sponsoring thought. We can create anything we want here in heaven. Our religions have created major sponsoring thoughts for the world; one of which is that we cannot truly experience peace until we die. We think that when we die, we will be happy in heaven. Well, I choose to be happy now, creating the life I want to live now, leading by example and helping others to see how they can live the lives they want to live.

So, how do you remove sponsoring thoughts? By coming to the realization that your beliefs are just that — beliefs; limitations on what you can do, on what we can do. By reading books, speaking to people, watching TV, or any way you can experience life, you have access to more information. The more information you come across, the more insight you get into what you choose to believe and what you choose to manifest. The key is to understand that you choose what to manifest by focusing your thoughts. Ask yourself what it is you truly want. Focus your thoughts there. Remind yourself every day of what it is you truly desire. Feel as though you already possess it. You have already become it. I changed my sponsoring thoughts on everything. I chose to remove them and let Spirit guide me. I accepted I know nothing, allowing myself to recreate my sponsoring thoughts. One by one, they began to change. I ceased to manifest things I did not want. Everything I wanted became everything I had. I felt as though I already had it. I watched it manifest. I practiced gratitude for everything every day, continuing to thank God in advance for what I was manifesting.

With this concept of feeling as though it is already so, we can answer the question "how do we shift out of the main reality?" With great focus and understanding of how our thoughts create reality, one can focus on being somewhere else. You would release everything from this reality and place your focus on having lived in another reality, fully believing it is possible. You can switch timelines in this reality, you can go to other planets, you can leave this body. Astral projection is something many people have accomplished. In going to another reality, we would have to come back to tell someone, and that person would have to believe us. Anything is possible, and many people have accomplished reality shifts. It is merely a belief that you can, then doing what you feel is necessary to complete the shift.

Chapter 8
How to Reprogram the Reality We Reside in

This time, when I am talking about the reality we reside in, I am referring to the reality you create, not the reality we collectively create. It is the reality you believe to be true. What you experience daily depends on the foundation you have created. This comes from listening to positive affirmations, taking positive actions, and removing negativity from your life.

I started with listening to positive affirmations on YouTube as I worked and while I slept. I would put on an eight-hour video of positive affirmations instead of listening to music. I would hear, "I am strong, I am worthy, I am important, I am love, I am smart, I am abundant, I am living the life I came here to live, I am doing amazing things, I am a kind person, I help others, others help me, I am beautiful, I am full of unlimited potential," and so on and so forth. All sorts of amazing things to input into your computer self. Even if you are not actively listening to them, your subconscious mind is. The more it is being repeated, the more you reprogram your mind. Think of it as tally marks for how many negative and positive things you hear in your lifetime. If you have heard more negative, you will think negatively. If you have heard more positive, you will think positively. Listening to affirmations rather than music for a week should bring about substantial changes in your thought processes, and how you view yourself and others. You will even find yourself repeating the phrases from the videos or audio recordings. The more you become aware of positive shifts, the more positive shifts will occur in your life, and the more positive shifts you will create in your life.

Taking positive actions is something I started doing as soon as I realized how my actions affect others. When I say positive actions, they range from simple things to big things. Hold the door for someone, tell someone their hair looks nice, give money to a homeless person; these are simple things anyone could do. My grandfather who had barely any money to give was the first person willing to help anyone. I learned from him that it does not matter how much you have, you can still help. My grandfather's home was falling apart. The house had a hole in the floor where you could see the ground beneath. His house was also leaning to the left. I am sure there were countless other problems with the home, yet he allowed his daughter, her son, and one of his other daughter's kids who was almost 30 come live with him for free. He gave them money so they could get back on their feet. All while he lived in the situation he did. He did not complain; he helped others as much as he could. He talked about everything going right in his life and enjoyed the time he had. He went outside to feed birds and squirrels. He set a wonderful example of how one should live life regardless of one's situation. He never asked anyone for help other than God. He took what God gave him and helped others in any way he could. Now, he is living a much better life in an independent living facility. He was provided dentures. He was able to get new furniture. He is experiencing life from a much better foundation now. The essence of this story is, we can all help others, no matter the situation we are in. Whether we volunteer our time, our money, or our goods and services, we have a choice to help. We were created with love. We should express love towards one another. Do something nice for someone every chance you get, and God will make sure you get what you deserve one way or another.

The removal negative things from our lives creates space for what we truly want. When I say negative things, I mean everything and everyone bringing negativity into your life. Negative things could mean foods you eat, the music you listen to, habits you have formed, TV shows you watch, toxins you put into your body, friends who gossip, or anything you feel does not align with your moral code. Sometimes, it is better to remove yourself from a friend group if they enjoy doing negative things over bettering themselves. Before removing yourself, take the initiative and show them how to be more positive. I do not mean to call them out by preaching your point of view on positivity. Start doing positive things around them. Choose to no longer partake in negative conversations. Lead by example. Complimenting what they wear is an easy way to start. Focus on the positives always. Anytime a negative comes up, remove yourself from the situation or change topics.

However, I must warn that as your friends see you become a better person, it may cause tension in your group. They could want whatever it is you have, or they may try to bring you down. You can only help so much before you must leave. Sometimes, we can help them become more positive with us. Other times, we surround ourselves with nicer people. You are who you surround yourself with. Look at where your friends are headed in life. Is this the life you wish to live? If so, then keep up the great work. If not, make changes. This is your reality; you get to choose how to live it.

I had to leave my friend group, and I found plenty more along the journey. As I continue to better myself, the right people come into my life at the right time. I am much happier with the life I am living now. I can be friendly with everyone and make much better connections with strangers. I am free to be myself. I am happy by myself or with others. I remember the life I came here to live, and now I am living it. I have several people in my life that I am close to; people I can share my thoughts with. These people care what I have to say, and I care about what they have to say. We have created wonderful bonds. I happily call them my friends; friends who are eager to hear what I have to say. I would prefer to talk about spirituality, creating reality, the law of attraction, karma, how we will live life, how we can help people, and how we can better ourselves. I love being asked deeply spiritual questions. Ask me questions about the universe you cannot find the answer to. I will do my best to find an answer we can agree on. I could go for hours talking spiritually. People like me are out there. Perhaps you are one of them who is also looking for people like yourself. Trust the process. The right people will come at the divine right time. Stay faithful.

So, how is this reprogramming our reality? After doing these three things, you will notice you have more positive thoughts, nicer conversations, and have new people in your life. All will lead to different and better experiences than you were previously having. As I mentioned in the last chapter, you could travel to another country to shift your reality. This would move you into another reality. In this situation, you stay in the same area but still change your reality, thus, reprogramming the reality you are experiencing. If you remove the negative foods from your diet, and you replace them with healthy foods, then you would eat at healthier restaurants, no longer eat fast food, cook at home, and maybe eat dinner with some of your new friends. All of these are different realities you can choose to subscribe to. You can choose to walk a different path than you had before. You can make the necessary changes to better yourself. You can create a better reality. Positivity makes way for amazing opportunities to present themselves in your life. If you are on this path already, you know how much better you feel. You know where you have been, how you used to think, and how external events used to affect you. Look at you now, living the life you came here to live.

Chapter 9
How to Fix the Reality We Have Created

To fix the reality we have created, we have to look to our master manifesters. Children believe almost everything they are told by adults. We put them into school at a young age to begin programming them. Sadly, at the time I wrote this, they were being programmed to be employees. They were not taught how to work for themselves. They were not taught how to find their passions. They were taught that they must go to college so they could earn higher paychecks and receive benefits. They were taught that the world is a scary place. They were taught that you cannot make it on your own; that there were bad people who would screw you over. This way of thinking creates a reality where kids believe they must complete college so they can work for a corporation in order to live a happy life. By virtue of this belief, what is created is a world where bad people exist to make working for yourself more difficult, where people steal, where people vandalize, where you cannot succeed without a degree, and where only working for those in power is what is safe. They brainwashed almost everyone in the school system to become worker bees for the man. I say almost because there were people who worked for themselves when I wrote this book. For those who did make it on their own with or without a degree, they became self-sustainable — not reliant on a paycheck to survive. However, they had to pay the government to support themselves. With this system, the U.S. government continued to pile on debt. What can we do? The only reason a government should be in place is to protect the people, not to pump out so many laws that people have no idea about unless they study law. This causes people to blindly follow the rules. With people blindly following laws, those in power were unable to properly finance the country. One can only remain in debt for so long before it is collected. The purpose for writing this passage in the past tense is to focus our energy on this way of living to be behind us. Focusing our energy on the new Earth we are creating.

What we do is show Adults how to reprogram their minds to always do good. However, their choices would only be good if they were programmed that way from the start. With this new Earth we are creating, we must have a way to show kids the truth. Help them live out their heart's desires. I assume someone reading will be more detail-oriented than myself; someone who could come up with an exact plan from this rough guideline I have provided. For this, I thank you for your contribution to the inhabitants of Earth. We should still teach the basic materials, math, science, social studies, reading, and writing. However, we should begin showing kids new experiences so they can find what they are passionate about. Perhaps they would spend two weeks focusing on different trades. Just the basics of each trade, as we are not trying to bore the kids with details of every trade. Based on the fact that each person is different, some will find these to be interesting. When a child finds what they are passionate about, they will tell their parents and/or their teacher about it. They will be given more information about this so they can further pursue this interest. This does not mean they must follow this path, as they will still be learning about other trades in school.

Apart from teaching them trades, they should be taught all religions and how to find themselves spiritually. Forcing them into one viewpoint is not fair for the child. They should be able to choose what path they would like to follow. Meditation and yoga should be made a normal part of their daily routine. Set aside time for them to meditate each day. Have a yoga class at some point during their day. We have gym class; it would be easy to add a 30-minute or maybe even an hour-long yoga class. Make the reality of yoga, meditation, and prayer a normal part of the daily lives of all. Adding these three things to school will allow for children to become much more aware of themselves and others without casting judgment. It will also help them create a society that aligns with Spirit rather than ego. They are the next generation. We may not see atonement in our lifetime. However, we can start the movement for atonement to be seen in theirs. Atonement according to A Course in Miracles is, "The Holy Spirit's corrective plan that undoes the ego."

Another important thing we should reform about the current school system is grades. We should not grade the kids on their performance. We should encourage them to keep trying, instead of telling them they are failing. This grading system causes children to compare themselves to others. No one should compare themselves to others. We should be focusing on who we are and how to express who we are. Teachers should be helping kids find themselves, showing them how to apply who they are to the real world. Show them how to get started with their role in life once they have found it, where they will set up shop, how they will conduct business, how to set up shop, where to get the needed goods, how to distribute their goods, how to provide their services to others, the list goes on. We would have teachers for each specialty. There will be people doing new things as well; those we would not have a specialty teacher for. For these students, we will provide them with everything they need to know to get started. Then, we will ask them questions about how they will contribute to the greatest good of all. Help them to refine their thoughts. Help them focus on how they will express the divine within themselves. In turn, they will continue to bring new ideas and creations into the world. The best we can do is help them find a way to extract the ideas from their minds. Then, we will help them formulate a way to get started.

With school reformed in this way, we remove the negative conditioning from the government-controlled school. People work for themselves rather than work for corporations. The people have the power again. When people can provide for themselves, they do not need the government to provide for them. We work together in perfect harmony to help each other out. If we do not program our kids to believe there are bad people in the world, we will not believe them into being. Since everything arises from our thoughts, we must remove the negative. We must focus on the positive to remove bad things from the world. Even the thought of needing a balance of light and dark is a preconceived limiting belief. This is our reality. We make it how we will. We can choose to live our lives with positivity. If everyone is on the same page, we can align the world to be this way. It will take some time, maybe a generation or two, but it can be done. We can create a perfect world if we so choose to, living together in peace and harmony.

How does this fix the reality we created? By fixing the school system, removing government, and choosing to create a more positive reality. We can think of this as removing self-imposed limitations and replacing them with positive affirmations. However, this would work on a much larger scale. This would require at least half of the population of Earth to be thinking the same way. The task now becomes how to reach at least half of the population. We can do this by spreading love and raising the consciousness of everyone we meet.

I implore everyone who has read this book to give it to someone else. Everyone who makes it to the end should be on the same page that we can make a difference in the world. Together, we shape the collective reality as we know it. I ask you to take some of the knowledge within the text to allow yourself to be a better person. Share your knowledge with others who are interested. Talk about how you can make a positive change in the world. Take action to make a positive change in the world. In case I have not said it enough, "All that we are arises from our thoughts." We are living in heaven and have made a mess of it. We can experience heaven in any way we wish. All it takes is one person to make a change. How big of a change can 4 billion make? The answer is however big they wish. We create reality as we see fit. The most important thing to remember is, our reality is never broken. Everything is always in divine order. What we think about is what is. Focus on the perfection that exists so that we experience life. Then, choose what you will create. Placing our focus on a world that is already living in peace, love, and harmony creates that world. With the heaven state of mind, we know this is a temporary experience we get to have. We can choose to be blissful and happy every day. We can also choose to be joyous and loving. We can view the population of Earth giving hugs and helping one another every day.

Meditate and visualize peace and harmony. Where we want to go is a place of peace, love, and harmony, meditate on it already being here. Live in this reality as it is already here. Lead by example and show others a better way. In doing so, the law of attraction works to create this reality. There is no need to teach anyone who does not ask. They will come around when they are ready. Continue to see them as though they already see it. Listen to your intuition and go with the flow.

When you see the world through the lens of what you want it to be, the law of attraction works, both on an individual and collective level. As I focus on peace and harmony, I shift my reality, and as a result, others around me begin to see the same thing. As everyone who reads this book focuses on living in peace and harmony, others around them begin to see the same thing. Collectively, we create a world where everyone lives in peace and harmony. By already seeing it, we manifest it into reality. The more people with this vision, the sooner it becomes reality. Continue leading life as a positive example for others. We need do nothing to persuade them to live this way. Simply live life how you want to live. They do the same when they are ready.

List of Names

I would like everyone who reads this book to write their first and last name on this page. I have left the last pages of the book blank. Please give this book to whomever you are prompted to give the book to. Giving is the ultimate sign of having received. If you feel inclined to buy the book again, please do so. I am grateful for your contributions. Whenever a book is filled with names, I would like the person who possesses one of my completed books to reach out to me, I will host a seminar in your area. Thank you for reading my book and thank you for being kind enough to give it away. I love you all. Namaste.

List of Names

List of Names

CPSIA information can be obtained
at www.ICGtesting.com
Printed in the USA
LVHW081500040422
715261LV00003B/200